i

Everything is a Choice

Rick Yee & Oren Cox, PhD

Table of Contents

CHAPTER 1: EVERYTHING IS A CHOICE!

YOU ARE AMAZING!

Now, take a second and think about how that makes you feel. Did you call bullshit? Did you already know that you were awesome? Were you accepting and in total agreement with this statement? Did it roll off of you? Since I don't know you, how could I possibly know you're amazing? Did you just read and disregard it because it's irrelevant information to you? How did you just take that statement? If you think about the way most people process choices, you may realize that you made one just now! From completely starting your life over, to something as small as taking a compliment—all things require a series of choices that you are capable of making, either on a conscious or subconscious level, which, if you take a second and think about it, is very awesome!

Change inspires choice, and choice inspires change.
Understanding this, empowers you to do either.

We have unlimited potential to do both good and bad. We can create and destroy; we can love, and we can hate. We can even change our minds, or we can do nothing. We are incredible, and we are most amazing because we are the only creatures on this planet who get to make decisions about everything! We choose how upset we get, what gift to send, whether to say thank you, to pick a fight, or to let it be. You have the choice to forgive, to forget, to let go, to hold on, to rebuild, or to burn it down, bitch and complain—or do something about it! Inside all of us is the ultimate superpower; the power to choose.

It is important to realize some simple things about choices. Probably the most important thing you should think about when making them is that choices don't care what you do! They are completely indifferent as to how you feel and which one you pick. Choices don't get mad at you, and choices don't give you accolades for making good ones. Choice has no opinion of right and wrong or good or bad. Those are just options waiting to be selected. There is not a good or bad unless you decide you don't like the consequences of your choices. One person's bad is another person's good. If you don't mind the potential consequences of your choices, whether positive or negative, then it's not as seemingly bad to you. One person may not want to go to prison while another is used to being incarcerated and feels better on the inside than on the outside. It's just perspective that changes if the choice is good or bad. If you break it down, people develop anxiety and stress over choices because of five factors: information, confidence, opinions of others, fear, and action.

In the next several chapters, I will outline these five factors in more detail. I'm confident that at least one of these, at some point, has applied to every single person who touches this book, even if each person doesn't take the time to read it (clearly a poor choice!). So, go ahead and read on to learn how to take control of your choices, or don't! Remember, your choice doesn't care what you choose; it's your decision to make!

Consequences and Outcomes

Consequences and outcomes; they're one and the same.

The word "consequence" often has a negative connotation in the psychology of human behavior. However, very simply put, a consequence is an outcome; it is the result (or effect) of a chosen action or condition. Consequences are not good or bad; they are determined by perception. One person's "bad" is another person's "I don't care".

Consequences are the results of the choices we make. Like choices, consequences don't care what you decide to do; they are simply direct products of your actions. Cigarette packs warn that smoking can cause health issues, but people still use them because they are addicted to nicotine and cigarettes often provide the smoker with temporary stress relief. However, the consequence to that method of relief will likely be emphysema, shortness of breath, and lung cancer.

If I choose to tell a man his wife is disgusting, and that he's a worthless piece of shit, I will most likely suffer the consequence of confrontation. This consequence may come in the form of a verbal confrontation or a much-deserved "ass-whooping." I created a negative action from my choice, and it is a possible reaction for me to receive a consequence in one way or another. A possible outcome could be that he agrees and laughs, or another possible outcome might be to fight. Now, if I am okay with a fight, and even if I were to lose, then the consequences don't seem bad to me. If I fully accept either outcome and am ready for even the worst of situations, then I am fine with the consequences. If I do not want the potentially worst outcome, I will then decide if it's worth the risk, knowing the possibility of an undesirable result. Mind you, being a jerk is not cool, so it's best not to be that guy, but that will be addressed in a later chapter.

When it comes to personal growth and development, we need to be present in the pain of our choices; we need consequences to remind us that what we are doing is bad or harmful. We also need consequences when we make good choices to reinforce that we've done the right thing. Touching a hot pot on the stove will burn you, so how many times will you be burned and scarred before you decide to change your habits? Being an arrogant jerk will make others avoid you and will cause you to lose those who were once close to you.

It's all cause and effect; you make a choice or take an action that creates an equal or opposite reaction. If you treat a person like garbage, don't be surprised if that person isn't there when you need them. If you don't care for your car; don't be shocked when it starts having problems. If you eat and drink sugar all day; don't be blown away by the weight you gain. The upside to getting what you give is that, if you treat people the way that you would like to be treated— or in a positive and loving way—the favor will be returned to you. If you invest your time in activities and actions that bring about the outcomes or changes you want; you will inevitably find the results you desire. For example, if we show up to work on time, do our jobs effectively, and have a good attitude then there is the reward of continued employment and possible advancement in pay and position. Of course, this is not an absolute as there are people who do this who are treated poorly and sometimes still lose their jobs.

Remember the accountability in your actions. Accountability works for positive choices, too; take care of your things, and they will take care of you. Pay your bills on time and you'll have excellent credit. Selflessly love as you would like to be loved and see it returned or demolished. Perhaps love is not a good example, but you get the point. You can find balance in everything if you are looking for it. We must keep a balanced mindset and approach to achieve harmonious lifestyles.

Rock Bottom

Hitting rock-bottom is an essential concept for personal growth. We do not change unless we are forced (either internally or externally) to change and hitting this stage forces us to do so. The introduction of new information must be presented to initiate a changed perspective. Resisting change can be a defense mechanism, due to our survival instincts. Hitting rock-bottom means that you've not made good choices, and because you've not been making good choices, you've been suffering negative consequences. Rock-bottom is where you end up when you can no longer sustain the harmful lifestyle you've been living for a very long time. Rock bottom is the moment you're looking in the mirror, and you know that things must be different.

From the moment you hit rock bottom, you become a different person. The triggering event could be anything; suffering a trauma such as a spouse being unfaithful; realizing that you no longer love your partner of many years; or an event that alters the entire dynamic of your life. After that event—you are no longer the person you used to be. It could be the instant you realize the person you're with is not the person you're *supposed* to be with; the moment you fall in love or the moment you fall out of love.

Sometimes you look in the mirror and realize that the person looking back is not mentally equipped to survive, or that is what we tell ourselves. You then make a pledge to yourself: "From this day forth, I will do things to change those situations."

For example, a person who has become disgusted with themselves, thus they are at their personal rock bottom, and so they decide it's time to quit smoking. Some will say, time and again, that they want to quit smoking, but they can't. There is a physical and mental addiction to overcome. The nicotine is eradicated from the body three days after cessation, but people continue to pick smoking back up even weeks after that nicotine has left their system.

Now, there are exceptions and commonalities for all things, so we know people who have decided to quit smoking cold-turkey, and people who have tried to quit for months or even years. The one thing I notice with all people who make it is that they recognize their problem, have become exceedingly frustrated with it and have hit a point of no turning back. I interviewed a man who tried for a year to quit smoking and was unsuccessful. He finally quit outright when his lung collapsed. That incident gave him a far more immediate result or consequence to his choices. He hit a point of absolution; a turning point when he had no other option than to change or else he would for sure be in excruciating pain, or he would die. I like to call it "Hitting Rock Bottom"—the spot where we are no longer enabled to continue an action that will have eminent detrimental, or very unwanted, consequences.

A crisis situation occurs when all the choices you have made accumulate and lead up to a negative circumstance; these choices are usually small and go unnoticed until you repeatedly stack them up in your mind. It is really an accumulation of experiences but one event that triggers change. Whether the rock-bottom moment is a lifestyle choice, a wake-up call or an emotional epiphany, it's the moment we realize that we have a need to change and the realization that we have a choice to change. In most normal, everyday cases, we find ourselves holding onto things from our past and forget that we have an option to look forward. Many people I have met feel defined by their past in a negative way and harbor those emotions as though the past is still ongoing. In many of the situations I have encountered, this defining circumstance for these people occurred years ago and had no application at the time or in the future except for occupying space in their heads.

These memories either leaves us with amazing defense mechanisms or massive barriers we construct so that we cannot let anyone close. When I was young, the house in which I was raised was plagued with very intense physical and emotional abuse. At that time, it was only my younger sister, brother, and myself. I, being the oldest, still remember it and had developed a defense mechanism where I could become emotionally detached from any situation. I was very much like a robot as a kid. I didn't know that at the time, but I was often indifferent and angry towards things, and that anger helped to guard against the abuse I was experiencing. The repercussions started to develop in my teen years when I became a byproduct of my environment; being angry and getting into fights. Basically, I was like the Incredible Hulk. All it took was a quick moment, and I would rage out as an impulse. I did something foolish during a meaningless argument with my high school girlfriend (who was way too good for me at the time) when we were arguing in the car, and I lost my temper and punched my car window out. She, like any sane person, was shocked and not okay with that behavior. And I remember getting out and standing in the shards of my window with blood pouring down my arm and realizing that I was raised and designed to be this. I was made to be angry; to break things; hit and scream. At that moment, when both her tears and my blood were hitting the ground, I realized what I was. I then had an option I did not know existed—to choose not to be what I was bred to be. I didn't ever want to cause the stress or pain that I created for her in that moment for anyone again. I made a choice that I was not going to be like that anymore. I had hit what most would call a "Rock Bottom" situation—the point when I had to embrace change.

The fork in the road was more evident than before. It was always there, but now the choice was much more apparent. I could just see the choice so much more clearly.

Rock Bottom is different for us all. We all have a past that was designed to mold or shape us into something we may not want to be.

The memories of the intense moments that have created us have shown us that we can survive anything. The shit you have been through, as Tony Robbins says, "happened *for* you and not *to* you." The moments that force us to see who we are in situations define our growth and allow us to recognize when we have opportunities to change or respond.

The beauty of hitting bottom is that it forces change. Change forces us to adapt and grow, providing new opportunities and outcomes. It is up to you whether you make a change for the better or worse. Most commonly, we lean towards survival, so our choices are influenced by what will help us feel—or remain—alive. Then, it becomes an issue of perspective...what choices will sustain our best idea of living?

The point of this is that I was able, at that moment, to recognize that I was not who I wanted to be. I could see a future of failed relationships and escalating self-destruction, leaving hurt and pain in my wake for beautiful people who didn't deserve it. I knew I would eventually project my issues onto someone and mess them up because I was not comfortable in my own skin, or happy with who I was. It is not worth the risk to let my upbringing and conditioning to allow me to be a violent and angry person left unchecked. *I* decide who I am. I decide how I want to handle things. I don't want to be angry. I don't need to explode. I choose to be patient; I choose a better way.

The same goes for you; you can choose to say, "fuck it", or forgive it. You can choose to let it go. Most of the time, the events that take place that help us change or grow come from the moment when we make the decision to change because we are accepting the circumstances and allowing change to occur. It may take hours, months, years...but ultimately it comes down to the moment when you say, "I'm changing this. Now".

Society urges us along by encouraging a similar idea in the form of a New Year's resolution. Every day can be a resolution day if you want it to be.

I have the power to do this; I am an evolving person with the ability to focus on a positive outcome as a matter of my free will.

No matter what gives you strength, use it: G-d, positive affirmations, laws of attraction, karma, balance, evolution. I believe they are all working together at all times and that these things are not mutually exclusive. Find your strengths and the empowerment to recognize the reasons *you* do things. Take action when you've made the choice of who you want to be.

There is absolutely no shame in seeking the help of a professional. Go to counseling for help in guiding you if you're lost. Associating yourself with more positive people can also be a massive help and a huge boost to your confidence. If you don't feel as though you currently have that confidence...fake it till you make it! Pretend to be more of who you would like to be until it becomes your reality. For example, many people believe that they smile because they are happy. This is mostly true, but it is not the entire truth. Research shows that smiling can help you to feel better; even if you have no reason to feel good in the first place.

"Some types of bodily feedback, such as facial expressions and expressive behaviors, are an important part of emotional feelings" (Laird and Lacasse, 2014, as cited in Lin and Gong, 2015, p. 383). This is an example of *fake it 'til you make it*; if we are unhappy but force ourselves to smile through that pain, it can have a positive impact on our psyche.

Decide on an image, an idea, of who you want to be and work to move toward that idea. Whether your goal is to be more patient, a better listener, a person who smiles more, someone who is easily able to enjoy things, or someone who can play an instrument. Choose a trait or skill you wish to develop and commit to yourself to doing it. When you can see your options, it is far easier to make a choice. The only things in your way are the excuses you make (likely out of fear) to take away your choices. So, recognize your excuses, decide that you can do what you want to do, and the *way* to do it will present itself—if you are looking for it. If you believe you can find the path to your goals, or that you are your own path, then do so; otherwise, if you believe there is no path, and you are looking for all the reasons you can't achieve your goals, then you won't. Either way, if you focus, you'll find the things for which you are searching.

We attract what we are focused on because we are looking for those things. I encourage people to watch or read *The Secret* to understand how the mindsets we choose matter and will produce the outcomes we desire. All things are connected, and all things work together at all times.

The Law of Attraction is very similar to the act of praying. The idea in many religious groups is that if you pray enough and believe in the outcome you are asking your higher power for—you *will* be rewarded with it. With the Law of Attraction, positive thoughts reel positive events, feelings, people, and situations right into your life. If you believe you are the one in charge of your destiny, then you have the power to make your destiny something fantastic. Embrace the fact that empowerment is your right if you choose to embrace it. The Law of Attraction is when two similar things attract each other; "like attracts like" (Atkinson, 2012). For example, positive thoughts cause positive outcomes and the same idea goes for negative thoughts. Focus on your vision and whether G-d delivers it or if the universe is at work, it will still have the same outcome. If you believe you make your own destiny, then make it a good one. Embrace the fact that empowerment is your right if you choose to embrace it.

Justifications are worse than excuses; justifications are often far-reaching supportive reasons that twist something we would typically be uncomfortable with into something that is suddenly acceptable. Justifying negative actions to avoid consequences is a tactic that even "good" people employ to try and alleviate the consequences of their actions. That, or they support and "understand" excuses given by others to let them continue to make bad decisions. For example, "Oh, he had a rough childhood," or "he's too old to change." "Well, if they didn't do that thing I wouldn't have to…" all are paper-thin justifications not to take personal accountability for the decisions we've made.

Even when we choose to do nothing, that is still a choice, but to ignore or discredit our options is to choose to fight our design— our ability to make decisions and grow from our problems and mistakes. Living in the problem is unhealthy and usually leads to isolation and negative attitudes. It makes us develop defense mechanisms that trigger lash-outs or snide remarks towards anyone trying to alleviate the problems; "Oh, like you could ever understand my problems! Have *you* ever had it this bad?" It's a habit of constantly looking backward. Deciding to stagnate—or not to move in a positive or forward direction—creates a negative, heavy feeling that becomes a daily battle to overcome. This lifestyle becomes a rut you can't shake if you continue to employ the use of excuses and justifications.

But the upside is that if you are (or were) this type of person, now you'll be able to pinpoint two hindrances in the decision-making process, and you can identify them, squash them, and move forward (to the next chapter).

Indifference

Being indifferent toward outcomes allows you a clear thought process regarding how to handle them; anything in excess will yield an unbalanced result. This can potentially include good things you love, for example; dancing, watching movies, playing a videogame, working out, or wave-running. Do any such beloved activities repetitively, for twelve hours a day every day for a year and see how much you like them then.

Without balance or varying stimulation, we get exhausted, bored, or even start to dislike some of the things we once loved. Just ask most people what they think of their jobs. Do they like the work they do? Do they find it fulfilling? Meaningful? Probably not in most cases. Put in sixty hours a week at a job for a decade doing the same thing, day in and day out, and you are very likely to become burned out. (Of course, people who have found a balance within themselves, and who are engaged in an occupation they love, can find and maintain a healthy work-life balance).

It is crucial that we go through the pain of making and suffering the consequences of our own poor decisions because they help us to grow as individuals, and they give us the wisdom to make better choices moving forward. People who have been through tribulations often have a very different view of problems than people who have suffered very few struggles to contend with throughout their lives.

It's frustrating to see parents who want their children to be better than they are but at the same time, those parents do not allow their children to have the experiences that will make them who they will be.

Our mistakes, pain, the bruises, the falls, the shocks, and the surprises—are what make us "us". The challenges we endure, and the hardships we survive, help shape the way we see things. This gives us our own unique perspective on how we decide to handle our trials and what we feel we deserve.

A person who has suffered through a tough childhood, intense relationships, or any difficult life situations, will look at small problems such as a broken shoelace, a bad date, or a spill on an outfit as trivial and they will be able to quickly move past such incidents. Such incidents are nothing compared to the deeper pains a person who has truly suffered has overcome. However, we have all either seen—or have been guilty of *being* the person for whom a horrible date or making a mistake at work has interrupted and ruined perhaps a day or two for us. All of us have allowed a small error or mistake to metastasize into something we've agonized over for far longer than we know is good for us.

It's only a mistake if you don't learn anything from it.

Perspective

To convert my weaknesses into strengths, I consciously made a consistent effort to overcome my defense mechanisms and programmed rage. I found that the safety measures and survival tactics I created just to make it through the crazy days could be altered into tools of productivity. I'll explain.

Instead of never experiencing emotion—or experiencing too much emotion—during the times when it would have been overwhelmingly painful, I found I could practice. I could take control over my emotions and how intensely I allowed then to effect myself and those around me.

For extenuating circumstances, like fights or other confrontations, I could turn off my feelings either, to better rationalize or to protect myself from hurtful words in arguments or life situations. This helped me to see more clearly. I'll admit, this is not always healthy and has taken years of practice. But what else was I doing that I didn't have time to do that, right? That being said, when used as a superpower, it has come in handy in extremely stressful situations.

On top of controlling my Hulk tendencies, I had to develop a very high patience to be able to keep "The Monster" at bay. The trauma I had been through made typically stressful situations much easier to cope with in comparison. When others would panic, I would remain calm and steady.

In my personal experience, everyday stressors weren't very intimidating compared to what I had already been through in my life, so many other situations felt like much smaller issues. You, too, have been through worse than most of the problems you face on a daily basis and you'll also be fine after those problems are solved and have passed.

Again, I took my biggest weaknesses and chose to convert them into a very high tolerance for bullshit and a more open perspective for solving problems. I recognize that, had I not hit rock-bottom with my anger issues, then those simple, every day stressors would still reduce me to a raging mess. Once, when I was at work, a lady stole my chair out of my office and I freaked out. She lied, saying she didn't know what happened although others saw her take it. This caused a rage within me because of prior experiences of people taking advantage. Hitting rock-bottom forced a positive change within me.

The point of my story is that my issues were programmed into me from childhood. I was taught behaviors and reactions to situations that became a part of me. I had every opportunity to make excuses and justifications as to why I inflicted the damage I did, and some might even be accepting of it because of my past.

I was able to choose. Now, I can decide what I become. I can choose how to handle my problems, and how to treat the people around me. I can choose to be something different than what life predetermined I should be up to that point.

I can beat any internal problem if I decide I want it gone. I can turn my weakness into a strength if I can identify it, I can *choose* to get rid of it.

Making Choices

I know that my method of processing choices might not be the answer for everyone, but that doesn't mean it's not productive for me. Remember, choices don't care if you do something or not. There is no one-size-fits-all when it comes to anything. You have to learn to know your choices. This is one tool in the toolbox of what makes you "you."

I have developed an ability that I can use, but this is not how everyone works. That's why the choices for help, like psychologists and therapists, are an option to assist you to train, understand, and control your powers. Psychologists and therapists may not be the solution for everyone, just like my methods may not be the solution for everyone. But that doesn't mean that if you're struggling with mental health that you shouldn't seek help from a professional. It's often much healthier to see a professional than to try to deal with serious mental illness alone.

The principles I've outlined here are still valid (at least for me), and the making a positive change or meeting that goal of who you want to be—can be accomplished. So, use the suffering of your past. Use it to help you create defenses that will protect and aid you, but don't allow that suffering to define you as a human being.

We can be hurt, punished, abused, abandoned, betrayed, neglected, and berated. But we also have the power to stop the cycle with us; to not continue it throughout our lives. You don't have to be a product of something negative that happened to you—you aren't made solely of tragedy. It's the mixture of tragedy and beauty that make a whole person. Due to the horrors you have lived through, you have the tools and the ability to recognize such craziness from a mile away and choose to either avoid or embrace it. You can turn the sins of the past into a positive future by merely choosing to do so. It starts with an understanding that there is a decision; that no matter how trapped you may feel, that you *do* have a choice. You always have a choice.

To do this on your own is a difficult task. It takes a lot of self-reflection, self-discipline and courage to go it alone (this is discussed later). Draw on any resource you can to help guide you, be it professional counseling, a psychologist, family, friends, religion/faith, self-help books, a mentor, a life coach, or an image of a role model you would like to emulate—anything that will help encourage you to keep growing. Use any or all of them.

As I've said, we have powerful abilities to protect ourselves and to make our own worlds bend to our will. It will take practice and time to hone your powers. The more help you choose to accept, the faster you will grow and the more you're feel like you want to continue to grow. You will no longer feel the way someone has told you to feel, or the way you've been primed or conditioned to feel. You really do have a choice!

A wise person once said, "The definition of insanity is doing the same things over and over and expecting a different result."

There is nothing wrong with knowing—and understanding the impacts of—your past, so long as that knowledge and understanding is used as a means of growth or a tool in learning to move toward your future. But constantly looking back will stagnate any movement forward you would like to make. You will consistently miss amazing opportunities because you are facing the wrong way. The past is gone—it's over. Yes, it's still a part of who you are, but you can't change it. Your options are to learn from it or to let it control you negatively. Mistakes are only bad if you don't learn from them.

We are powerful. You are just as strong as you can imagine and as resilient as you believe... you only must make the choice to embrace it all.

The Race to Acceptance

Recall the five stages of loss and grief: denial and isolation, anger, bargaining, depression, and lastly, acceptance, because that is the most relevant topic here.

In the race to acceptance, the main thing people struggle with is change. With either new information or a change in their physical world, people find themselves struggling to accept that the initial changes have already happened. It's hard to look at one's ever-evolving world and say to oneself; "Well, this is it. Better just roll with it."

The race to acceptance is an understanding, or perspective, that allows you to quickly and healthily get to the point of making peace with a change that has already occurred.

The real struggle we face with any choice is that it most often involves substantial, personal change. *We* must alter ourselves to effectively adapt to the evolution of our lives. Luckily, humans are a very adaptable species. Change is one of the biggest fears people face, and every time a new introduction of information enters our lives, we are required to make new choices. For example, I was once offered a lucrative job at a medical university, but I would have to risk leaving a secure job and my spouse would have had to leave her business behind. This was one of the most stressful events we dealt with because we feared that change would cause negative things to happen; losing what we had, and the possibility of putting ourselves in a bad financial position if the job didn't end up working out. Another example was when I had to divorce my first wife, she was abusive and was cheating so I had the choice to stay or to leave. The hard part was making the decision to leave and it ended up being the best choice I could have made. It all worked out in the end.

How are we going to handle these things? Do we allow our emotions to drive our actions? New information means change, and change is scary. Just about everything that has to do with choices also includes personal changes. So, the real struggle in the race to acceptance is to accept that things *must* change even though you may be resistant to that change.

We're all guilty of the prevalent misconception that change is bad when; in fact, many times, change is simply the unknown. We subconsciously fear the unknown and the unknowable. It raises our hackles; induces panic.

Ultimately, however, we must accept external changes for better or worse because even the most horrifying, blind unknowable can morph from a black hole of fear into an actual evolution of the self. That unknown result of whatever change you face could end up having a positive impact upon your world.

Change inspires choices and choices inspire change;
understanding this empowers you to do either.

Now, for significant events like loss of a loved one, it's important that you go through the stages of grief at a pace that's comfortable for you. The time frame for healing from a traumatic event is different for each person. For the emotional part of this, I would recommend reading books that help with handling that kind of loss. Some examples include any books about death and dying by Elizabeth Kübler-Ross or *The ABC's of Healthy Grieving: A Companion for Everyday Coping* by Harold Ivan Smith.

Accepting that something has already happened and being able to train yourself to acknowledge your responses and recognize that you have a choice, gives you the ability to avoid reacting in a fashion that brings about negative consequences (big inhale). While that mouthful is accurate, the point really comes down to; you can't change what already has taken place. Since it already *is*, what's the point of constantly upsetting yourself thinking of what might have been or how you might have avoided the situation?

Here is a logical answer: it is pointless to get mad when something is not what you imagined it would be (we will get into this more in the next chapter).

When someone or something has occurred and has lodged itself under your skin or has upset you—you can accept that it has already happened and that you can't choose (or change) the past. You can then decide what you will do to move past it or respond to it. Instead of dwelling over the make-believe version of what you wished would have happened, focus on how you will reconcile and manage what has *already* happened.

A wise man named Randy Wiley once told me, "control your controllables". Move to acceptance as fast as you can. If you made a mistake, then you made a mistake! Take what you've learned from making that mistake and learn how not to repeat it; *learn* from your mistake. Eventually, with time, any witnesses will forget about the event. Own your errors and move on. Personal accountability is a massive advantage, and a trait that garners respect.

The absolute best thing you can do in a tough situation is to respond appropriately and move past it. Doing your best is not necessarily about speeding through the process, but an approach of healing as quickly as possible can help people move toward the acceptance phase rather than getting stuck in an unhealthy loop of not being able to move forward.

When one doesn't manage their problems in a healthy way, that can lead to deeper problems later on because the issue was not fully resolved. Such issues remain unresolved when a person doesn't give themselves the necessary amount of time to internalize his or her feelings. We do not simply get over something easily, but we can find ways to help ourselves move along healthily and happily. While breaking a problem down to the simplistic version of what it's truly about, try to be indifferent about it, and weigh out your options.

Belief Systems

Belief systems are a sensitive topic if you choose them to be, and you might not agree or be able to handle systems that differ from your own. Remember, this is one perspective, and it is not labeled "gospel" on the cover. So, relax because disagreeing is perfectly fine.

Now, I don't know your belief system, but I know that what you believe is correct at this point in your life. Personally, I believe that everything in our universe works harmoniously to create our existence. Everyone, no matter their religion or lack thereof, is right in one way or another. I do not pick sides, and I do not judge others based on their beliefs. You are free to think and to believe what you wish to think and believe. It's simply a waste of time to argue that a person is right or wrong when neither of the people involved in the disagreement can provide tangible, objective proof to support their claims. It's easier to go about believing what you wish and respecting that others will do the same. I find it difficult to disagree with any belief system. Why would it matter when we all end up the same in the end?

We are all here on Earth together and want what's best for ourselves and our families. Yet we often draw solid lines in moving sand, and we pass judgments on things that aren't any of our business; things we cannot control.

Most of us are simply trying to procure and maintain safety and happiness for our loved ones. No matter what belief system you adhere to, you would likely agree that we are all creatures created the same. So, why do we worry about our differences when we're all made of the same stuff? Especially when the real differences between one human being and the other are rather insignificant?

If you are not religious or do not believe in theories like the laws of attraction, karma, evolution, or reincarnation; that is fine, but these philosophies can be helpful if used as a lens to help better understand choices and outcomes. As humans, we are advanced by whatever power you believe put us here, and with that advanced status, we get to shape our lives by making decisions every day. We are able to adapt, learn, and evolve from situations and grow past life's obstacles in the process. Being adaptable is pretty amazing and we should find our adaptability to be empowering. We cannot underestimate our abilities and resilience. You are stronger than you believe.

If you believe in the G-d of the Abrahamic religions, then you know that we were created in His image; unique and with Free Will. We were designed to make choices, but also to make mistakes. I often see people of faith looking for confirmation, be it through prayer or through seeking signs, that will let them know that what they are doing is right; however, this often looks to outsiders like an excuse to not do what you were meant to do. I believe G-d gave you the ability to think, so you can use the gift he gave you to choose. He is curious to see what you do; make an excuse or take action by doing what you believe is right. This is often why when we are in limbo on our decisions, in many cases, these are the times we are the most uncomfortable.

So, instead of waiting for a sign to do something, imagine just thinking of the action as the sign you've been waiting for, and you'll be able to give yourself permission to make the choice/change you desire.

The bible and many accounts of history are filled with stories about the consequences, rewards, and decisions our ancestors made so that we can make better ones. This does not, of course, mean that every impulsive response you have is right, but we'll get more in depth with that later. The one thing I know is that when Jesus shows up in the Bible, he makes a point that it is not for us to judge the fate of others. If you feel it's your place to determine whether someone is going to heaven or hell, or that it is your place to say, then you must believe that your deity upstairs is not as capable as you are in determining that for himself/herself. (Pending your view).

The next time you choose to be vicious to someone in your creator's name, pause to ask yourself a few questions. Did Jesus kill and attack people? No. Shouldn't you be like him? Yes, that's the idea. Maybe we can look at coexistence as a choice. We are all put here by the same source and just want what's best for our loved ones and ourselves. We will all be judged in the end by something greater when we die. So, it's possible that not making everything suck for everyone around you is an option you can choose, too (just like being a piece of shit).

Stop Bashing My Shit and Move On, Please

Look in conjunction with how the laws of attraction work (*The Secret*), which specify that what you focus on, you will find. If you look for negativity, you will find it; if you look for the good in things, you will also find them. If you focus on something coming to you in your life, then it will find its way into your existence. Some people call this prayer, and some call it meditation, but no matter what you call it we send a signal out from us that is powerful.

Have you ever felt someone staring at you from behind you; feeling a hole being burned in your back? Have you ever randomly, out of seemingly nowhere, thought of an old friend whom you've not seen for ages, only for that person to reach out to you within the few days that follow? This is the embodiment of the idea that we send out signals into the universe, which then brings whatever it is on which we focus into our lives.

This applies even if that on which you focus is not necessarily a good thing. For example, if you're running a bit behind in the morning and you're driving to work. During that stressful drive you repeatedly mutter, "I don't want to be late. I don't want to be late.," and somehow, despite how desperately you don't want to be late, time seems to magically go by faster, simply to spite you, and suddenly you're pushing to be on time to work, or you're pushing to just be a bit less late. While it's the outcome you did not want, you were still focusing on being late, so you were late. You were focusing all your attention on being late and you didn't even know it. Changing your focus changes what you will find. Next time you're running late, try telling yourself: "I'm going to be on time. I'm going to be on time". It shifts your focus to a more positive mode of thinking, and also changes the outcome. It's a silly example to help you understand what I mean. I encourage you to read, or at least watch the documentary of *The Secret.* It will open up this powerful philosophy.

Other things we have heard (or have even said ourselves) include, "I'm not going to get that person to want to date me. I'm not going to get that promotion. I'm never going to lose this weight. I'm never going to have any money," and you see the pattern. Negative thoughts will generate adverse outcomes. By recognizing that you have a choice in the things that you say to yourself, you change the outcome of what you will receive in your life. You can do this by just tweaking the words slightly to say, "I am going to get that person to want to go out with me," "I am going to get that job," "I am going to lose this weight no matter what!" or "I am going to find a way to make more money." The ability to choose to change the outlook you have on the problem now opens up an entire avenue of solutions and possibilities that were never there when you were not looking for them.

What you focus on is what you'll find, and what you focus on is a choice.

The concepts of karma, evolution, and balance work hand-in-hand with the ideas of G-d and with the laws of attraction. All things are not separate or independent, but all things work together to give insight into the way you make choices. This means it's not about right and wrong but a choice that we accept the consequences for because it seems there are consequences for just about all beliefs. So, in the words of Trent Reznor of *Nine Inch Nails*, "Bow down before the one you serve. You're going to get what you deserve." The point is to have your beliefs because you are allowed to choose your faith just like others are free to choose. I believe it's not for us to judge (we all have our own judgment waiting for us in the end), but for us to accept that we are all here together. So why be an instrument of hate when the act of accepting others will not hurt you? Living with love may make you feel good about your actions! Surely it doesn't make you feel good to hate and judge?

If there is to be a fate or judgment, let the G-d or greater being you believe in do the judging and appreciate that we are all made by the same source, whatever you choose to believe exists. We can all learn from each other, be it from our similarities or differences.

Notes & Thoughts

Notes & Thoughts

CHAPTER 2: ACCOUNTABILITY

Believing that everything is a choice allows you to take full accountability for your actions. After all, if you did something, well… you did it. No point in denying it out of some vague sense of "pride". If you get hurt doing something foolish, either physically or emotionally (or both), own it. You chose to put yourself in the situation or not to prepare yourself for it.

If you've said something harmful that you didn't intend to be harmful, or if you feel like you could have handled a mistake or situation better, the odds are that you could have. Like all things, it all depends on how you look at the incident in question, and one small bit of perspective or information can change everything.

There is a school of thought that I've encountered; it maintains that *everything* is your fault. What does that mean? Well, it would mean that if you were attacked by someone, and you never learned how to defend yourself, then the results of that attack are your fault because you never took the initiative to learn how to protect yourself. You know there are martial arts classes you can take everywhere. Let's say you've been unable to save money and then an emergency occurs—an expensive one—that requires a ton of money from you to resolve. Guess what? That misfortune would also be your fault because you didn't learn or care to save money in the first place.

Often, we tend to blame others for the negative aspects of our own lives, and that results in us being hurt because we are not taking accountability for our own lives and that prevents us from moving forward. Sometimes we'll even find scapegoats for *our* reactions towards *them*. I'm sure you've either uttered or heard something like this before; "If you didn't make me so mad, I wouldn't have to say things like I did!" We all have room for growth and we also have the ability to build people up or tear people down. You get to decide if your people in life are having positive or negative impacts, and you get to respond accordingly.

You have more control than you think. If someone is hurting you either physically, emotionally, you do have a choice. You don't have to suffer what you've suffered. I understand the fear of loss, loneliness, and the unknown. I also understand the fear of retaliation. So, it's the frog in boiling water; put a frog in soothing water and slowly increase the temperature, and the frog will stay in the water until it boils and dies. Put it in hot water to start with, and it will jump out.

We'll look into fear and self-reflection soon, but if you're being harmed, please try to recognize your own free will and your own choices. You *can* make a better life for yourself.

Excuses and Justifications

Everyone can have a reason why it's okay to fail!

Excuses are so damn easy to use. There will always be a reason *not* to do something. If you want to lose weight, you can come up with a million reasons as to why it's not doable for you at the moment. "But, it's hard."

To succeed at almost anything, repetition and self-discipline are required. Getting in better shape, being a better dancer, reader, painter, builder, bowler; the list is endless. To choose *not* to better ourselves is to choose to fail. Every day, every person has a laundry list of reasons he or she could pick from to not follow his or her goals.

Oftentimes, humans can get caught up in a cycle of victimhood; "look at my problems. Look at my problems. Look at them!" and fall into a rut where he or she is *living* in the problem. Many people have a story about how bad their circumstances are, but they never really ask questions (either internally or externally) that could help them better those circumstances. Even if a viable solution is presented, it is often ignored or discredited. Sometimes we believe the problem is so overpowering that it becomes our identity for a while. Sometimes, the bitterness of pain suffered in the past is all a person allows themselves in terms of self-definition.

We all either know a person—or you might even be the person—who constantly sees the world through the pessimistic outlook of "The cup is half-empty." Because misery loves company, you will sometimes hear people (not everyone), use their sorrows as a cry for attention. They want to evoke pity so that they are given something in return, whether that something is a get out of jail free card, a ride somewhere, money, getting out of an argument, being excused for a poor work performance, etc.

I've also witnessed people lying to gain recognition in other ways when it would be most beneficial to directly state the issue. For example, when you're discussing a particular issue of yours, or a problem: something that is bothering or upsetting for you. Perhaps you're with your support system, a group of mostly sympathetic friends, but there's always that *one* guy (or gal) who just can't let anyone get away with having greater hardships than they experience. So this "friend" tries to one-up you in a twisted sort of misery Olympics (a game you had no desire to play in the first place). So, you know that person might say, "Oh, you think *that's* bad? Listen to my problem..." It is very rare you will hear the one-upper share a solution they are working on for the issue or, any movement on improving the situation about which they're bitching.

> *"My health problems are so bad..."*
> *"I wish I could quit smoking!"*
> *"My relationship is so stressful..."*
> *"I hate my job so much!"*

Now some people choose that misery-loves-company lifestyle, and that's fine, too. If you love being miserable.

So, when such a person presents problem after problem to which you offer solutions; that advice will fall on deaf ears. Because they don't *want* help. They want pity or attention. In most cases. The seemingly obvious advice of, "Seek counselling for you and your partner, or get a new job then!" is often followed up with an excuse. "Oh, you don't understand; when it's good; it's so good." "Well, that happened only a couple of times."

Now, I would like to say that relationships are tricky, especially ones in which one person (or both) are suffering physical or emotional abuse. So I would advise anyone reading this book to never ignore a friend who may need help in that regard. They will be inclined to give excuses as to why they can't just leave their partner. But those excuses aren't the type of excuses we're really discussing here. We're talking about folks who likely exaggerate or even outright lie about their problems to seek attention. If you suspect someone is lying about physical abuse within a relationship; it's always wise to take them seriously even if you doubt they're being honest. Offer them support and any resources you have, but please understand that your friend will have to recognize for themselves that their partner is abusive before they will be ready to leave.

If your friend makes excuses to stay in an abusive relationship, those excuses are likely rooted in fear of what would happen to them if they were to leave. Bodily injury or harassment are not uncommon reactions from partners who are abusive when the abused party finally decides they've had enough. So be supportive of any friend who is in such a situation and be patient. Because sometimes it isn't as easy as "just leaving" a person who has beaten you down to the point where there's nothing left of the person you once were.

Ok, that being said, let's get back to the liars and one-uppers that you're trying to help!

Reason after reason is given to why the options or choices are not valid and cannot be implemented. The excuses are seemingly endless, too. Excuses keep the choices we have from becoming an option. Sadly, most excuse-driven people will just politely accept (but never heed) the suggestion you give and move on to the next person to dump their problems on and to listen to their stresses.

Oddly enough, we often accept negativity and excuses openly. If it will not affect you directly, then there is often no reason to get involved. If it's not yours to fix, then let it be broken.

Excuses and justifications are hazardous things. They allow something we know as bad or wrong to become acceptable. However, the harder choice—the choice to change, or to move on—while being difficult to make, is often the best choice. It's unfortunate that some don't recognize their own free will.

Excuses stunt our growth, and justifications provide us reasons to live in the past. Soren Kierkegaard said it best: "Life can only be understood backward, but it must be lived forward." How can you grow if you are continually dwelling on the past? The past is over, and you're wasting precious energy that you could use in the present. Yes, it's good to know where you came from to have an idea of where you want to go, but the most important thing to remember is this: where you came from does not dictate where you are going.

Excuses are extremely common, as demonstrated in everything from continuing a bad habit to abusive behavior. We cite reasons why excuses should be accepted—and not rejected—We always give ourselves reasons to accept excuses and procrastination. We accept these excuses because we have become complacent. We're not necessarily happy, or even content, but we *are* comfortable. Even a negative familiarity can be less terrifying than change. Often, we are flat-out hateful in the process of self-talk while we would find it unacceptable if anyone else spoke to us the way we speak to ourselves.

"I am a gross fat ass!"
"I am too ugly!"
"Why would anyone want to be with me?"
"I'm too poor."
"I can never be as good as that person, so why even try?"

You've heard them all before, perhaps you've even said them yourself. Regardless, these statements are merely excuses for not putting yourself out there, trying something new, or moving past your self-defeating attitude. It takes effort, but unfortunately, most people choose to remain comfortable in their discomfort.

Justifications are also incredible. Human beings are capable of extreme good as well as extreme evil, so long as we can find a way to live with whichever one we choose. Justifications are not a moral matter of right and wrong; they're just the things we tell ourselves so that we can live with our choices. It's easy to throw accountability away and justify your behavior or mistakes by finding a scapegoat and blaming anything other than yourself.

"I would not have done (insert whatever stupid/selfish/idiotic thing you've done) if you didn't let me or make me!" In many cases, people will do just as much as they believe they can get away with. That's why the world is full of rapists, thieves, and murderers. Ill-intentioned people are everywhere. But there are good-intentioned people as well who don't bring harm to others because they have a conscience that wouldn't permit such horrible acts.

If you find yourself struggling with what someone else has done, it's because they believe that the consequences don't apply to them, or they decide that the consequences for their decisions are wholly acceptable. Here is an example; a couple who live together break up, and one moves out. One takes things they want that they know are not theirs. I have seen it referred to as "asshole tax", or "bitch tax" but, ultimately, it's the price a person pays when they know their stuff is lost for good, not that the other person has necessarily stolen it; just that it wouldn't be worth it to see that person again in order to retain possession of their belongings. Even though the action is something they don't want done to them, they find ways to rationalize why their choice is OK; why it's just dandy to do to someone else. The consequences don't apply when I've decided that (and rationalized why) it's ok to steal.

Justification enters the picture when we tell ourselves that our choices are fine because we've earned our behavior. We're owed a debt. There are many justifications for any situation, and they can all be powerful. Justification gives us the ability to do the things we do, whether good or bad, and not completely implode on ourselves. We reconcile our actions with our conscious in this way.

Understanding justifications gives you a different perspective on how you will choose to handle someone or a situation, knowing that your intent and/or survival instincts are to find a way to cope with the choice, the outcome, or the consequences.

Responses and Reactions

The most important thing isn't really about what terrible things happen to us, but how we choose to handle them. Becoming a person who *responds* instead of *reacts* is a choice. You don't have to remain the person you have always been. You can take responsibility rather than blame. You don't have to get rage-monster upset. Instead, calmly find a solution. You get to choose how to handle any situation. Understand your choices in situations and also learn the difference between responding and reacting.

Reaction

Reacting is more of a knee-jerk reflex response to a situation. Getting upset, name-calling, throwing things, panicking, hiding, or losing control, in general, are reactions. They are impulsive actions performed without thought or reasoning. Impulsivity can become a trained response that is taught through conditioning (or lack of appropriate conditioning). It's how you immediately respond to a situation when it comes to handling problems.

Due to nature, among other aspects of our internal computation of external stimuli, we are conditioned to react to situations, as well as to the consequences which we have been taught can be either good or bad things; these experiences directly affect our perceptions. If you don't get into trouble for acting like a crazy person, or the potential consequences don't have any impact on your decision, then you're being conditioned to believe that it's not going to be a big deal if you act out with violence or extreme anger. If you don't suffer negative consequences from extreme behavior, you may feel that perhaps hurting others isn't a bad thing because it's not affected *you*. But this is very rare mindset. Most often, we learn *some* level of accountability and self-reflection.

People who react subconsciously (or in extreme fashions consciously) are not aware of (or don't care about) the consequences their actions until it's too late to change them. They can be a whirlwind of destructive actions, and when the smoke clears, the people around that destructive person are often able to see the devastation that person has created. The party who is in the wrong will either move on, leaving a mess in their wake, or ask for forgiveness *after* they've caused harm.

Such toxic people usually live lives filled with excuses and reasons as to why it's okay (or *should* be okay) for them to do such horrible things to other people. Those reasons can often sound like this; "I had a tough childhood," or "You don't know what I've been through." They will often use your decency against you by hoping that because they've revealed their trauma to you, that you'll excuse the trauma they inflict. The sad thing is that this strategy often works, and most of us have encountered it and been a victim of it.

However, not all reactions are bad; if you train your body to react positively, then you will create favorable reactions. There are many tricks and possible outlets to accomplish this, such as engaging in a physical activity or a hobby that calms you (cooking, painting, martial arts, meditation, weight lifting, running, etc.). Learning to focus on yourself can help to raise not only your awareness of, but your patience towards, trying situations. Sometimes, it can help to take yourself out of the situation for a moment and do something else with your brain. Something that doesn't involve hurtling a chair across a room or slapping someone in the face. The next time you find yourself yearning to react to a situation in a negative manner, try focusing on your breathing. Take slow, deep breaths. Count to ten. If the situation involves a heated argument, you could take a break from the conversation to decide how to talk about it calmly.

If you lose your cool and just start breaking things and hurting people in an Incredible Hulk rage session, such a negative reaction will most likely result in negative consequences. (Unless you don't want people around you, then that's how you want to behave, and the resultant lack of friends is an added bonus.)

During an impulsive response, you allow your emotions to take the wheel, and instead of acknowledging that you have a reaction issue, you fall back into excusing and justifying why your horrible reaction is either okay or someone else's fault. With that sort of behavior, you are ignoring that you should blame yourself and you are justifying that you just *rage monster'd* all over the place (yes, *rage monster'd* is a real thing, I checked).

Responses

Responses are different from reactions because a response requires an assessment of a more desirable outcome based on the choices we make. We take a moment to decide how we want to interpret a given circumstance, and then make the best choice based on the options we present ourselves. A response is a more measured, less impulsive form of a reaction. When we respond to something, we take the time to *think*; to weigh our behavior and actions.

Responding (rather than reacting) makes it easier to keep a sound, balanced mind. We can then foster a more informed mental environment in which we can find a solution rather than create more problems. No rage monster here, unless you decide that the best outcome for a situation is, in fact, to rage out. At least in weighting decisions, you know what you are doing and are aware of the potential outcomes.

Responding makes it easier to find a compromise and balance in a problematic situation so that you can create the results you would prefer. Couples fight over money, past relationships, lying, weight loss, family, etc. These are all resultant of reactive behavior rather than responsive behavior, and reactive behavior in a serious relationship only creates poor communication and a flailing relationship without balance.

Having a *responsive* conversation dynamic without name calling or harsh, impulse-driven words makes it much easier for any couple to overcome their problems together. Or even, *gasp*, admitting when you were wrong in order to move forward—is a choice based on responding rather than reacting. Both options make it much easier to examine the problems and choose solutions *with* each other versus *against* each other.

Simplify Your Choices

When you don't understand what your options are or when you have too many options, the overload causes anxiety and can make the process of producing a decision confusing and overwhelming. Often, when overwhelmed, we take no action, which causes even more anxiety. Or we second guess (even triple guess) the actions we take, which freaks us out even more.

Studies have shown that the more options you have, the more overwhelming the choices can become. I highly recommend the TED talk by Sheena Iyengar called "The Art of Choosing". If given ten options to choose from, most people don't make *any* decision and instead simply walk away from the situation. For example, if a person has ten choices of which jam to buy, studies have shown that it becomes overwhelming and most people decide that maybe they'll just have the PB sandwich without the J.

But when only two or three options are available, people tend to choose more easily because there aren't as many opportunities for them to make the *wrong* choice.

This works in all aspects of life. If you can assess your situation and condense your options down to two to three for your best-case scenario outcomes, this takes a remarkable amount of pressure out of the equation, and you're less likely to make a potentially wrong choice.

I have found that the best way to avoid negative outcomes is to narrow down the number of choices. Even better if it's possible for you to nail down only two options. These options should be the two outcomes you are the most comfortable with. If you're comfortable with either one, that and the overwhelming feeling of anxiety will be easier to overcome than if you had twenty choices to weigh.

The genius concept of simplicity is easily overlooked because of the gravity we individually tend to ascribe to our problems.

Like Tony Robbins said, "Accept the problem as it is, but don't make it bigger than it is."

Every problem comes with options, and sometimes the best options aren't great. But, to sit in them is to let insecurity and doubt creep in, threatening to dictate what we do next, rather than implementing our free will. It is fear and doubt which make us stagnant and immobile. In short, it makes us go crazy.

Look at the problem, recognize that it's there, and then choose the best way for you kick that problem out and move past it.

It seems so simple that it's almost silly to talk about our problems (especially the one that are more complex than they may appear on the surface) that way, but simplicity is genius. Keep it simple. I love the principle of Occam's razor – "the simplest answer is usually correct." Once you can recognize the hindrances in your decision-making process, you will be capable of responding with great ease, having eliminated the extraneous worries from your past.

Now, I know this notion sounds cliché and absurd because you didn't choose for your family member to get sick; you didn't choose for your office to be downsized; you didn't choose for your house to catch fire. However, it's more important to focus on how we are handling the situation rather than what the situation has done to us.

I'm not suggesting that every situation is a Mentos commercial moment (even though that would be awesome!). Many problems can be solved with creative ingenuity and confidence. I am not necessarily saying they can't be. I am saying that no matter the process of your decision-making, *you* get to decide, and you are not helpless. For instance, let's say two drivers, both driving identical cars, hit some black ice and smash head-on into a pole (in an identical manner). The airbags deploy, and the cars are totaled. Both drivers received minor cuts and bruises, but they were both lucky it wasn't a lot worse. Driver one gets out of the car, looks at the damage, and gets mad as hell. "This is great! Just great! Now my car is ruined! I'm late for work! Going to miss that meeting! My insurance is going to skyrocket! Now I have to take the day off to fix this shit! Who puts a pole here?" All he can muster is complaint after complaint about how much everything sucks, pouring negativity onto anyone and everyone. Oh, and I bet everyone he sees that day is going to know about it.

Driver two, in that exact situation, gets out of the car and realizes that he probably should have died just then. He starts reflecting on the last thing he said to his loved ones and stupid grudges he held that would have meant nothing if he would have died there. From that point on, he starts to tell others who he believes deserve appreciation that they are appreciated and spreads love to those whom he loves. Every minute from that moment on is borrowed and cherished and should not exist for him. The dreams he wished he pursued, and the goals he had nearly amounted to nothing. His life was supposed to be over, and he now has a new, positive outlook. He has a second chance to do better, which makes every second he lives a gift, and that's why it's called "the present".

Note that the circumstances weren't better for one person than the other. Both cars were destroyed, and both people were banged up in the same manner. The only difference was how the situation was *perceived*. This is an extreme situation to some, and some of us have been through much worse than a little old car crash. However, that's the point; it's all perspective.

We will have problems we must grow past and overcome. I read a quote that says, "People always complain that life is hard, but what are they comparing it to?" Not life. Now, the interpretation of life can range from how you tied your shoes today to overcoming issues from your childhood or negative relationships. We always have a choice in any given situation, and we must make choices every day—some are just much harder to face than others.

Whatever gives you the empowerment to push forward—G-d, science, fate, chance—whichever you choose; can be a source of strength for you to harness so that you can move forward. Everything works together in a balance whether you choose to accept it or not. Embrace the power you have to make a better life one small choice at a time. Every small choice adds up. This concept is called "Slight Edge" thinking, and it originated from an author named Jeff Olson. It's a good read, and I would suggest it to help with personal growth.

"Slight Edge" thinking explains how, at first, the inches we move are almost not even noticeable, and our choices seem like they don't even matter. But, sticking to achieving the goal, inch after inch and choice after choice, everything adds up and compounds over time to cover a great deal of ground. You will grow leaps and bounds and be in a much better place than you would be if you chose not to move forward at all. You may perceive that no change is taking place because the change itself is small or because it doesn't occur instantly. However, I want you to go back and reflect on past struggles you've faced that required a series of decisions. Think of each choice you made that helped you to forward, and then think of how those decisions built on each other to lead you where you are right this moment. You have a lifetime to reflect on, so go ahead, I'll give you a minute. Think about health, wealth, love and happiness.

The accumulation of these life moments gives us choices and finding the most graceful way to handle a situation is not always easy. In many cases, the problems we face are not easy, but there is a graceful solution if you only seek to recognize the option for it. We should strive for grace in our solutions and project the outcomes we would like to create instead of simply further acting upon a wild impulse reaction. Learn how to respond instead of reacting, so that you can improve the outcomes of your decisions and limit emotional setbacks.

Notes & Thoughts

Notes & Thoughts

CHAPTER 3: EXPECTATION AND INDIFFERENCE

Expectations are a tricky thing. They are one of the things that people get the most upset over without even realizing it. In almost every case that I've come across—in interviews and in life—expectations come from an idea of what we *want* or *imagine* other things or people will be like, and we get upset when the reality doesn't match what we've envisioned.

Oftentimes, we justify our expectations out of some sort of fanciful entitlement, which is kind of fucked up because what we want things to be isn't always how or what they are. And some things we simply cannot will into being. "I was promised this." "I was told by someone else that you would do this." "I was hoping this would happen my way," or "I wanted you to be like this." Sure, we've all had these thoughts, but our desires can't always change reality. Expectation changes the way we accept what's happening around us or *whether* we accept it. "They told me I could get a discount." "I can't believe you lied to me." "You aren't showing me the attention I want." "Well, so and so does it this way, so you should, too." Think of all of the weird things we say to deny what's happening in front of us because we made believe that it was going to be different. Use the race to acceptance here.

These perceptions are very different from our standards. Standards are levels that we hold ourselves to and the parameters in which we find things acceptable. Standards are where we find our non-negotiables and the means by which we determine whether we should put up with other people or stay in certain situations. An expectation is something we engender with our preconceived notions; it's a thing we see in others or a thing we wish would happen that may not. A standard is how we hold ourselves accountable.

Say I am a person who wants to be in shape, physically, for my health, so I work out at least three to five days a week. I watch my diet, and I do certain activities to obtain and maintain that shape. I do those things to reach the standard that I've set for myself. My expectation (once I've met that goal) is that I'll be able to compete in body-building tournaments within three years. That expectation may be somewhat reasonable. However, if I have the expectation that I'll be able to get greased up and flex in front of an audience within three weeks; that's an unobtainable expectation.

Relationships

There are many types of relationships from family, friend, lover, etc. However, romantic relationships are by far one of the most common situations in life that require a constant string of choices (made by both or all parties) in order for the bond to develop and flourish. I would also be so bold to say that I am sure many of you picked this book up hoping to find tactics on how to cope with your own romantic relationship(s).

I don't know how invested you are in your endeavor to change how you make choices, but for this section, you might want to grab a pen and paper. Write down the things you want, the things you don't want, and if/how you are willing to compromise in your current relationships. This can help you gain clarity and a different perspective So, let's start to break this down.

In the dynamics of relationships, it often seems that at least one member of the duo tends to either consciously or subconsciously try to change the other.

Those who do this subconsciously don't realize they are doing it. The idea that the person you are with should begin to fill a purpose they were never intending to fill (or even knew would be required of them) creates frustrations that should and could be settled through compromises, not arguments. Expecting a person to change into something he or she did not agree upon, or even know that you wanted or needed them to be, will create tensions in the relationship's dynamics. The idea of accepting your partner starts to get harder because they are not growing into what you imagined they would/should be, or they aren't doing it at the speed you expected. These expectations are a deteriorating catalyst that only serve to ruin our romances, friendships, workplace dynamics...any form of relationship.

Now, this is not to say that you shouldn't have *any* healthy standards in life. Everyone should seek characteristics in their friends/loved ones such as minimal kindness, or not waking up to a screaming match every day (but hey, if you like that, I won't say that it's right or wrong). However, if you think about it, non-acceptance—or imagined expectations—are genuinely what breaks down a relationship. Example time? You bet! I will give you a simple one. Just remember, while your problems may be different, the principle is the same:

Alex and Sam have been in a relationship for just shy of the three-year mark. Sam has never been the "acts of service" (e.g., doing the dishes, taking out the garbage, etc.) type, and it has never really been required of Sam. Alex has always taken care of Sam, and it has not been a problem for Alex because Alex is a "giver." (Please hold your judgments...insert whatever lifestyle choice that applies to you or your loved one.)

Until, maybe one day, a conversation with a friend or notable influence highlights that their partner is a dish-washing machine who is happy to take out the garbage for them.

Perhaps The Giver just doesn't feel like doing the dishes anymore and suddenly decides that unsuspecting Sam is not pulling their weight and needs to step it up. Whatever the reason, coming home one day and seeing dishes annoys Alex more than usual. This annoyance ferments until the fateful day Alex blows up and confronts Sam as to why Sam hasn't done the dishes. Alex's not-ready-for-this conversation partner, having not had any indication of Alex's new desire, now has to defend against a dishwashing version of themselves that Alex has, essentially, made up.

Alex is frustrated because Sam is not going along with Alex's new desire; Sam, on the other hand, has no clue why Alex is mad because Sam has never been the person who Alex is suddenly claiming Sam should be. Now Sam becomes defensive and in direct competition with an imaginary version of themselves who, in Alex's mind, is a "better" version of the real Sam.

Now, maybe Sam starts trying to do the dishes, but maybe Sam doesn't. If Sam does start to do the dishes, then it reinforces that Alex can simply change Sam into whoever Alex wants because Sam has shown a wiliness to go along with anything Alex blows up about. Sam's not absolved of wrongdoing here, either because Sam is rewarding Alex for blowing up instead of communicating. If Sam does not do the dishes, then Sam's inaction will only perpetuate a constant stream of not measuring up in the eyes of their partner. This couple will certainly have recurring arguments.

The choice is Sam's, but the problems will keep coming. Why is Sam's dirty laundry next to the hamper? Why can't Sam fold the laundry like Alex wants? Why is the trash not out at the exact moment Alex expects? Why don't you like my friends? Why don't you ever do things for me like that couple on TV? So-and-so's partner takes them out once a week, so why can't we do that?! This list becomes exhausting! It's an ever-evolving, uphill battle of a huge lack of healthy (and simple) communication. The idea of changing someone or *expecting* them to change on their own without knowing that the change is what their partner desires, is flawed from the start. It's like getting mad at an apple tree for not making bananas.

Regardless of the gender of the antagonist, the principle is the same. Expectations without compromise, balance, and communication, cause one party to constantly try to live up to the other's ever-evolving ideas of what they think they want. It's the opposite of growing together as a couple. There must be an acceptance involved. Both parties must communicate what their expectations are, and what they will not accept.

You can communicate and grow together, accept who you are with, or even conclude that your partner is not the person for you. It is imperative to understand that it's okay to not be with a person with whom you are incompatible.

I repeat, it's okay to not be with a person who is not right for you! I so often see people fight to save a one-sided relationship that completely lacks a balanced dynamic. Where there's a decision to either settle or deal with someone who is not willing to compromise with you.

It is also important to know that you may meet someone with whom you click on many different levels and is a seemingly wonderful match, but whom you don't need to try to change into someone you think will make you happier. Both parties should remember that to be with each other is a choice, and not being with each other is also perfectly okay option to choose. As human beings, we are constantly growing or moving in our lives. Sometimes that is a good thing for a relationship, and sometimes it isn't.

Acceptance is the key to not having so many judgments and expectations for someone else. Being able to accept another person is very hard if you're constantly passing judgment and looking for the negatives. It's a self-fulfilling prophecy—if you are looking for someone to fail in a certain area, or just "waiting for the other shoe to drop," it often will. What we focus on is what we will find. If you are looking for problems, you will see them straight away. This concept works the same when a person is looking for positive things about their partner. For example, in a fresh, brand-new relationship, it is often easy to overlook character flaws in the other person because you are seeking so much of the good. They may seem perfect—their appearance, their sense of humor, their nerdy comments, their contagious laugh—the list is endless! Due to these "New Person Perfection Goggles," we often make deviations from our normal criteria or standards because the positives you see outweigh the negatives (at first). I have witnessed the patterns of people who consistently date then later "discover" problems in their relationships that were either always there or otherwise self-inflicted.

Traits or hobbies initially praised and celebrated, in the beginning, can evolve into a "problem" in one's mind. This "problem" could be a hobby or a habit that was present when you met, such as playing video games, smoking, creating artwork, exercising, spending time with friends, guys' night, girls' night, playing Dungeons and Dragons—it doesn't matter. Any activity that a person engaged in when you first met, or spends time doing without you, can seem like a positive at first, or at least it can be viewed as not being a problem. Until you come to a point where your expectations change, and your previous acceptance disappears.

We start to crave more attention. We want something that somebody else has, or we just want to change things up because the monotony of how things have been starts to bore us, and we can't continue on that way.

With this new change in acceptance, whatever that person's "thing" (hobby or activity) is, that you originally found endearing, suddenly becomes a source of contention. Arguments ensue as to why the offending party won't stop doing the "thing" that was a defining part of their lives before you met (hell, it is part of what made them the person you liked so much!) simply because you either decided that you *don't* like them spending their time enjoying their "thing". You stubbornly refuse to join in said activity, perhaps due to the amount of attention it takes away from *you*.

Often, the hobby becomes a problem because the annoyed party does not have his/her own "thing," and so he/she views any lack of quality time as an issue because he/she does not have a passion of his/her own on which to focus.

If you your own hobby that makes *you* happy and that happiness isn't contingent upon whether your partner does it with you; it's far less likely you will become upset or feel slighted over your partner doing something that makes *them* happy.

If you have a problem with the person you are with, and not just a direct opposition to their "thing," you get to choose how to handle it.

Choice one: you can take interest in their outlets of enjoyment and identify something you can do together through practice or encouragement. Choice two: you can find something of your own that makes you happy and does not require your partner to give up the thing they love!

If the hobbies your partner chooses create a dynamic you do not want in your life, then perhaps consider that his/her choices are not for you, and no compromise can be met. That's okay. It is also okay for you to not be with that person! You get to choose!

If you are not as compatible as you had hoped, don't stress about it. There is someone else out there who will meet your needs and grow with you; don't be afraid to venture away from something that is not working in order to find that person.

Of course, you should try to keep a balance and to work on things first. Don't just fly right to divorce or break up with someone the first time something doesn't go as you hoped/imagined it would. If an interest that is not able to be shared takes all of your days from each other, perhaps you need to make a conscious choice as a couple to find a mutual interest you both enjoy. Take accountability for your choices, but also accept your partner's choices.

We all know someone who over-invests their time in television, work, video games, or whatever it is they are most interested in. There is nothing wrong with this if it makes them happy! If you are with a person like this, and you spend all day at work and then all night on a video game, and you have no interest in spending time with your significant other, then perhaps it's time to evaluate if this is the person with whom you want to be in a supportive relationship. You aren't giving up. You're just choosing to be real with yourself and to adhere to your own standards.

Intelligent Resource

Now, this part is a big fat key in evaluating efforts, communicating, and making informed choices in a relationship. Are you ready? Here it is: I highly suggest making sure that you are able to recognize your partner's love languages. I would suggest researching love languages to gain an in-depth understanding of your own language, your partner's language, and how they work together. One of the best resources on this topic is *The Five Love Languages: The Secret to Love that Lasts* by Gary Chapman. Just to touch on the topic (seriously, folks, read this book), love languages are the ways we interpret the actions or words of others in terms of romance and also the ways in which we show a person that we care deeply about them, and the method of expression is certainly not the same for everyone. Understand and accept that the thing that may fill your metaphorical cup may not fill your partner's. Recognize and appreciate that the way you show love—touching, acts of service, vocalizing, gift giving or quality time—is being given back the way you need it, and that your partner is getting the same. Having different love languages does not mean that a relationship will not work out; it simply means that you need to make an attempt to understand your partner's love language so that you can meet his/her relationship needs and recognize how he/she is showing *they* care.

First, you should figure out for yourself what expressions of love make you feel good. I'll give you a brief rundown of the several types of love languages. If verbal communication is important to you and you're the type of person who needs to express your love verbally and you also need to *hear* that you are loved, then you and your partner should embrace this need. If you are an "acts of service" lover, you're likely to perform actions to show how much you care. Such actions can include; making the bed, cleaning the house, cooking, fixing the brakes on the car, or taking out the garbage. Even the smallest of acts can show the person who values them that you care.

Do you show love through touch, or do you need physical reminders of affection from your lover? Backrubs, holding hands, cuddling, kissing, hugging. Hell, even a perfectly executed high-five can make someone who requires this feel secure or appreciated.

A gift giver will buy things to show that he/she is thinking of you, be it a shirt, a toy, a diamond, or even some completely random trinket that means nothing to anyone but the two of you. A gift is how the person says that you are important to him/her. If you appreciate quality time, you will just want to be with the person whom you adore. Activities, such as watching a movie together, trying a new hobby, or just being in the same room while you each do your own thing, can still feel good, so long as you both chose to be doing separate things together.

If one person in the relationship loves to touch, and that's how they say, "I love you," and the other is more verbal and actually says it over and over, it can leave both parties feeling empty when their love is not returned in the same way in which they express it. The *Vocalizer* may not like to be touched as much, and the *Toucher* might not like hearing "I love you" over and over. This disconnect creates frustrations because each party feels a sense of rejection from the person for whom he/she cares. Sadly, this feeling of rejection is unfortunate and totally avoidable. It's unfortunate because you are both showing the other how much you care; you're just doing it in a way that only you understand. If you like to get gifts as a way to say "I love you," and you are with someone who is not into gifts, have a conversation so you can define together what fills both his/her cup *and* yours. Without knowing how to make each other happy, you cannot choose whether or not you will try to speak your partner's love language. I believe most people would choose to do so in order to keep their partner and themselves happy.

The problem with mismatched and unspoken love languages can become a problem if you expect your partner to express love in a way that they don't know you need. You may also begin to imagine that your partner knows what you need; they are simply choosing not to provide it. It's a dangerous way to think. The fictional version of them (where they do what you need them to do) becomes more appealing, and the real version has almost no way of keeping up with the imaginary, upgraded version. Take some time to learn and accept each other and study the topic of relationships and love languages so that you can understand yours and your partner's. That way, you and your partner will be able to choose whether to adhere to those needed actions/words/touches so that you both have the opportunity to make each other happier. Read *The Five Love Languages* with your partner.

It's Not Me; It's Them!

Now, as prideful creatures, we humans will break out our *blame throwers* for relationship pitfalls centered on choices. Often, people who try to change others are unhappy with themselves. The people who most wish to alter their significant others usually have issues themselves that they choose to overlook or wish to not think about. To avoid any level of self-reflection, such a person instead chooses to focus on even the most minor issues they can find within their partner.

Changing others gives them the sense of empowerment that they lack in their own lives. As a result, in an effort to avoid their own shortcomings, they put all of their energy into fixing or influencing their partner to become something different.

Most Projected Changers would never openly admit it, but we find that it stems from more the profound need to fix something *they* deem broken, often something that is not even within their control or doesn't belong to them. "It's easier to have you change for me than it is for me to change." No, people don't typically state this out loud, but it's a pretty spot-on sentiment. Pride and ego play a huge role in these dynamics, and many people I have talked to feel it's their job to "help" their partner become "better". They operate under the false assumption that changing that person is "better for everyone." However, this "Operation Change You for the Betterment of Humanity" project is often not even made known to their partner. Or humanity.

If we are the target of this projected effort, byproducts of these selfish advances cause us to compromise who we are and that compromise will leave us unhappy, broken, or unfulfilled. One person often surrenders to try to make the other happy, and the other feels even less satisfied the more he/she tries. It's a dangerous cycle that people repeat over and over, and yet still, incredulously, they wonder why they can't find any "good" people to be with them. Well, champ, no one *wants* to be treated like a project, and that doesn't make them a bad person.

Objectivity is a powerful tool for you to use to assess your choices. This is also where your writing utensils can come in handy; listing what you want/don't want, see/don't see happening, or can/can't compromise on makes things pretty black and white! Then look at your list as if you are advising someone else. See how the answers change from when it was you who had the problem. Because we tend to give objective, fair, and decent advice, but we struggle to follow it ourselves. By employing objectivity (the ability to detach yourself from an emotional choice) and understanding what choices are best for you, you will be able to understand *what* is right over *who* is right in a given situation.

Look at the decisions without fear and anxiety over imagined outcomes and decide what would be best for you and the parties involved. Mistakes are learning opportunities—provided we take the time to learn from them.

The first step in the process to change negative patterns usually requires you to do the hardest thing in the world: take your own advice. Many of us can look at someone else's situation and know exactly what the right thing would be to do. We are able to give fantastic advice, but to take that advice ourselves? Forget about it! "But it's hard because you don't know him as I know him..." or "You don't understand; she does this because blah blah blah..." Yeah, yeah. I hear you. However, if those are the thoughts jumping into your head *now* over your personal relationship issues, you may want to go back and revisit the justification chapter. No worries— I'll wait for you. Seriously, don't stress about it. We have all been guilty of this one. Choices are often easier to hand out than to live through. We have to take the time to realize why we are choosing to try to change a person we care about and then talk about compromises in a way that will make both sides feel right about it. You need to make the choice to be patient with your partner when they are not perfect the first time. If change is necessary, be grateful for his/her efforts over the results. It was a collaboration of choices that got your relationship to this point, so wouldn't it only make sense that it would be the same process to change it?

Appreciation goes a long way and making someone feel good about their efforts makes them want to try more. This taps into The Golden Rule of treating others how you would like to be treated. You know you would not like to be made to feel like crap by someone you love trying to change you or keep you from doing something you enjoy, so don't do it to someone you love! Preschool classroom rules can follow us throughout life, eh? It seems simple, but we really need to watch ourselves during our growth to make sure we are not stunting it. Love who you are with for who they are, without expectations to change them or needing them to be something they have never been (or who you want them to become). Compromises are designed to be fair and help you grow together, not force someone to become an imaginary version of themselves. The beauty of compromise is simple; once you realize what you are doing (or what is possibly happening to you), you have the choice to find a better way through the problem as a couple, together. This will most likely require a mirror. First, look at yourself to know your own standards and goals, then determine how to compromise in a balanced way to make more room for the life and relationship you are not simply settling for, but that you truly want. I hope you have writer's cramp by now. Growth is painful, my friends.

Optional Examples

"My significant other just cheated on me."

Well, you can't go back and change the fact that they did it. That time has come and gone, so all you can do now is choose whether cheating is acceptable to you or not. A lot of times in such a horrid situation, you can just be thankful that you found out what kind of person your partner truly is, thus doing the heavy lifting for you. So, this way you can thank that dirty cheater because you're no longer going to spend the next few years investing in someone who's not going to treat you as well as you will treat them. Why would you stay in and watch nothing change?

Notes & Thoughts

Notes & Thoughts

CHAPTER 4: FACING FEAR AND HANDLING CONFLICT

Fear: an unpleasant emotion caused by the belief that someone or something is dangerous, likely to cause pain or a threat.

Personally, I have found anxiety to be an imaginary outcome of a possible future that has not happened and may never happen. Making it possible, but mostly make-believe or imaginary, it is natural for us to avoid things that make us uncomfortable or things that seem different because our brains are hardwired to keep us alive and to identify what is safe for us. We get this idea that if we live through something unhealthy and it doesn't kill us, it is okay. Even an unhealthy relationship is known as what it is; so, even though it's not good, it is *familiar*, and so it's better than the unknown. This is because what can happen in the unknown could be worse. This is opposite to "the grass is greener on the other side" analogy. So often, we stay in unfulfilling or even damaging relationships because we are afraid of loss. We feel that we have failed at something. We think that if we do something differently, we might lose this or that and the other person may not talk to us anymore. This is relative to the Sunk Cost Fallacy. Again, we fear the unknown. The fear of loss often paralyzes us into doing nothing or staying in a place that we know is unhealthy.

Like I said before, change inspires choices, and choices inspire change. Until we hit a rock bottom situation or have a moment of fearless action, we will not find the need to change. Until you feel the need to change your mind (or mindset), the mind will convince itself that it is okay to be there because you won't die from your less-than mediocre situation, although it may be killing you emotionally.

Fear has many faces: the future, the unknown, rejection, confrontation, change, embarrassment, success, or—for some—even happiness. We create these imaginary scenarios in our minds which are not the reality of the situation, but the worst-case scenario. Amusingly, these made-up situations actually control our lives. I've always enjoyed this topic when talking with people because fear levels are such an accurate measure of confidence and indifference to how people approach potential situations. When it comes to fear, it's often safe to stay between the lines because it's crowded there—that's where the majority resides!

If you feel unfulfilled by, or discomfort in not moving forward in life, I hope to help you address what is holding you back, why, and how to change your thinking to understand that it is no longer necessary. It's up to you to assess your fear and let it hinder you or propel you forward.

One of the most important ideas to consider when assessing fear is that one day, you are going to die. This is a fact. Pretty blunt, but really think about the implications of that. Of the fact that you'll die. Many people have a difficult time coming to the realization that we will all die and that we, personally, will cease to exist in our earthly bodies. We fear the idea of ceasing to exist as we know it; having to detach from our worldly possessions and loved ones. Once we realize our mortality as a reality, our concept of the things that we should or should not do changes dramatically. Things like time, procrastination, and excuses start to look very different when faced with a limited timeline. Seconds are how we measure the countdown until we take our last breath.

Your life could suddenly end at any moment. The person you're talking to right now may be the last person you ever speak to. You may have a car accident or have a heart attack at any point in the next few days, or even hours. The day a person dies can (and often does) start out just like any other, with mundane activities and interactions, up to the very last moment. We don't realize the fragility of life until we come to the conclusion that our lives will one day end. Sometimes we have time to prepare for death, and sometimes we do not.

It is important to recognize that this is our reality because the more we realize that we have a short amount of time, the more we realize that being afraid is pointless in the face of our dreams or ambitions. Many people at the end of their lives say they wish they would have worked less, spent more time with loved ones, and taken more risks. Get your pen back out and write down the answers to the following questions. Think about what holds you back. Think about what it is that *you* fear.

Is it failure? Embarrassment? Loss? Success? What makes you unable to resist change? What keeps you from doing what you know in your heart and soul that you should be doing? Going against our life purpose causes us to be in a state of disarray which can then cause us to become unfulfilled and lead to depression. Take some time on those questions. Write out what you believe the answers are and reflect on them. Look at the words and decide how terrifying the right thing really is to you. The thing we fear and that we fight so hard to accept is that, at the end of the day, nobody else really cares about what you were afraid of, what you did not accomplish, or what you did that's embarrassing. So, the value we place on the thoughts and acceptance of others who will continue to live their lives once we are gone now seems very silly. We all have our own problems and things to stress about, outside of the one-off situations from others' lives that don't actually apply to us. How many times do we stress about something only to realize that stressing over it was pointless?

Being able to live without fear and being able to rationalize the concept of stepping into a risky situation of, say, starting a business or following your dream, becomes a lot more urgent when you realize that you are mortal, and you only have a short amount of time here on Earth in which to do it.

You only get so many rotations around the sun to fulfill your goals and desires, and the people I know who fight their best to do the things that they are the most passionate about are the people who feel the most gratification in their days. Many people believe they were put here to do something more than just go to work and build somebody else's dream, while others make the choice to help their dreams become a reality. Neither choice is right or wrong, as long as it's what you feel is right for you. But it's best to follow what pulls you; we must follow our lives' purpose. You can choose your path based on fear or based on your own level of motivation to fulfill your goals.

Next, let's talk about excuses due to fear. The bottom line is that excuses are really just a cover so we don't have to admit that we actually have we options. "I can't dance," "I can't sing," "I can't play," "I can't learn," "I'm too busy," "I'm not that skilled," "I'm not like you," "I'm not smart enough," "I'm too short," or "I'm too good at thinking of excuses." These are all one in the same. Blah, Blah, Blah, Blah....all the reasons why we "can't" are defeating, but they are easy to list when rationalizing why you're passing on a growth opportunity. The next time you are faced with a challenge, for every "can't," list two reasons why you can. It's surprising how successful you can become when you have the "I can" attitude; however, if you end up not achieving what you wanted to gain, refer to the beginning of this chapter—you are very often the only person who gives your failures or mistakes more than a second thought. You can either quit, or you can learn from your failures and keep going. Everyone fails. In fact, you often must fail first in order to succeed. People suffer either the fear of failing, or even the fear of success and that fear often keeps us from getting back on the horse (or jumping on to start with).

So often we worry about what others will say or feel about us once we make a choice. We are so concerned about rejections and fitting in that we start basing our decisions on the (supposed) opinions of others, creating more excuses not to do what we would truly want for ourselves. So we lower our confidence while making a decision that should produce a great moment for us, and instead of experiencing a revelatory moment or a triumph, we watch ourselves miss an opportunity, and then come a slew of regrets; the whole would've, could've, should've feelings.

I want to point out that fear is not always a negative emotion—it can also a powerful motivator. Those who shy away from pain or discomfort are going to find being uncomfortable or being hurt far more motivating when it comes to making things better for themselves. It's easy to become complacent with not taking action to change when something is comfortable or convenient; however, sometimes the prospect of having the people around you suffer, or of suffering yourself, is more motivating than keeping things the way they are. So, it's the fear of a *worse* situation that can motivate some people to change their current situation

So, if you agree that, through being afraid of what basically amounts to the ghost of an attempt, you can shift your focus from "But, what if?" [insert negative outcome here that no one cares about] to "Why the hell not?" Now, no matter what you do, you can walk into it with confidence, and have the courage to make the best choices for you.

Recognizing whether fear stalls you or motivates you can be a powerful revelation. Too often, we find that fear paralyzes or immobilizes us to do anything that would be outside of our comfort zone. Most of the time, by pushing yourself out of your comfort zones and forcing yourself to feel even just a bit uncomfortable, you learn more about yourself and who you really are by facing and (hopefully) conquering that fear. Trying out for a team, giving a speech in front of a group of people, or dancing in front of a group— pretty much anything that would open you up to scrutiny and judgment in any way, shape, or form—can end up being your shining moment and reveal who you truly are as an individual. Being able to recognize a scary situation and to overcome it is one of the most gratifying feelings we can experience. Overcoming a crippling phobia can make a person feel the most alive. Once you are able to identify these moments (when you are faced with something that is potentially scary) and realize that the fear and discomfort is all in your head, you are then more likely to overcome it and make something amazing happen when you normally wouldn't.

In so many of our favorite movies, our favorite characters are the ones who are doing something courageous, scary, and outlandish, and we love them for that fearless behavior. There's no reason that you can't live your life that way, too—it's simply a matter of choice. Understandably, acceptance is a very, very powerful drug, and we all want to feel included and valued. The fear of stepping out and doing anything unique and not being accepted for it usually paralyzes people into staying in the shadows, instead of emerging into the limelight. You get to decide whether acceptance is for you or not.

You can create your own story or be a part of someone else's. At the end of the day, fear and holding yourself back due to fear, doesn't matter. The most tragic thing is that it won't matter either way! Someday you'll be gone and not as many people as you thought cared *will* care, so why base all of your decisions around the judgment of people who do not care for anything that does not immediately impact them? Even if stepping into a fearful situation goes (in your opinion) badly, more than likely, the witnesses will forget all about it by the end of the day. People are generally more concerned with what they personally have to deal with than dwelling on the words and actions of others. If you handle a failed attempt at something with grace and confidence, you make it easy to forget. Don't go beating yourself up about it. You tried, it didn't go the way you wanted, and you're still alive (I hope). The odds are you will be the only one who cares after the event, and that's often the worst-case scenario! Being courageous or cowardly in the face of fear is a choice.

On the flipside, the direct opposition to fear is courage and action. Courage is the ability to look at a potentially scary situation and do everything you can to conquer whatever fear you harbor surrounding it, and to overcome whatever stands before you. Courage is one of our most valued traits in society, and it is in almost every story we love. The greater the obstacle, the more we admire the courage to overcome it. A hero is defined by how they overcome fear to triumph over villainy and evil. That's why we love superhero stories so much.

These fears are exaggerated truths about huge problems that need to be met head-on in a glorious battle! The hero will take some hits and damage in the face of overwhelming odds, only to find the strength to power through, defeat the villain and save the day.

But our daily lives don't have to be a physical battle. Many battles we face are emotional, intellectual, or verbal. The greatest, scariest villains we will ever encounter are inside our own heads. Have you ever noticed that once you start doing something that was potentially difficult or scary that you started to realize it really wasn't that bad or that it was almost over before you get to the part you feared in the first place? With action, we become empowered and we realize that the problem isn't nearly as big as we believed it was. Turns out, our goal was completely achievable after all. With self-discipline and persistence, we *are* able to achieve whatever outcome we desire.

Think of a personal victory that once seemed impossible to you. Think of how you started really working toward that victory, putting in the time and effort to practice, or chipping away at whatever the problem or potential solution was. Likely, that scary. Impossible circumstance became much more possible because you took the steps to do it rather than avoid it because it was too scary. So, by combining courage and action, the things you were afraid of become smaller and smaller, and you become more powerful as you become more skilled and inch closer to your desired end result.

We are our own biggest critics, and we beat the ever-loving tar out of ourselves mentally. Our internal villain is a crafty one, too. Very convincing. In popular culture, we have personified the very dilemma of which we're speaking as the old devil and angel on our shoulders, each whispering their own poison or dreams into our ears. But, it is a real thing. Well, at least the concept itself is tangible. I often meet people who have an angel who can only whisper and a devil with a megaphone screaming at the top of its lungs. No matter how amazing we are, or how much potential we have, there is always something in our own minds at work to sabotage us. Humans are wonderful at self-sabotage.

Over and over in our heads, we say things that, if other people ever said to us, we would want to punch them in their hateful faces. The mind is the meanest and biggest obstacle people face. Once you identify where the thoughts are coming from, you can then make a choice to smack that villainous big mouth punk right in the kisser! You can choose to no longer be the victim. You can change how you look at a situation. You can change your mindset from "I can't" to "Hell yes, I can!" or my personal favorite, "Watch me do it!" Fear does not have to control you and should not be allowed to do so. It's not real! As soon as we can realize this, we will be able to make the choice to either listen to our inner voices (and more importantly, *which* inner voice), or not.

The Battle Against Fear

It is so easy to say, "I know I'm nervous/scared/afraid!" but to overcome any problem and move forward, you have first to identify the true source of fear which is holding you back. From there you can choose how you will respond. Henry Ford has a great outlook for this one; he would say if you believe you can or believe you can't, you're right. I paraphrased, but I find that most succinctly sums up how to overcome fear.

As I have seen Tony Robbins say, one thing that is missing in most people's choices to overcome most fears is certainty. In approaching a situation that you know for a fact, has a 100% chance of ending successfully if only you're confident that it will be successful, you'll find that success was inevitable. If you're able to visualize that your ability to do this already exists, and you visualize it over and over in your mind *knowing* you'll be successful, then the situation will follow suit . It is the concept of placing your mind over the matter and having complete certainty when approaching a situation that makes things possible and, in many situations, easy.

If you focus on your own certainty of success in the situation, then your body and mind will make it happen. Once again: what you focus on you will find.

If I know that I can lift two hundred pounds ten times, then I know I can raise the weight and still get at least a few reps. But, if I go into the lifting, looking at the weight, certain that it is way too heavy, then guess what? That weight *will* feel much heavier than it is. However, if I believe I can do that lift with 100% certainty, I will approach it with far more confidence. Knowing my ability versus the obstacle I wanted to overcome, I could choose to enter that lift with full confidence and the belief that I can do it. For all of us, as soon as we let fear creep into our heads, "This is too heavy!" or "There is no way I can do this!" that is exactly what happens—we make it real, and we drop our (metaphorical) weight. Whether you set your focus on what you want to achieve, or you believe you can't reach that goal, then that mindset will manifest as your reality. Zig Ziegler says, "If you aim at nothing, you will hit it every time." Truly letting fear creep in makes you feel like you have no choice and you will fail if you try, so what's the point? By now I hope you see that quote and think, "What's the point of being afraid?"

Closing Thoughts

In many cases, when attempting to gain something you don't already have the risk involved in losing something you never had is the same as if you try and fail. If you at least try, you are adding a chance for success that was not previously there. I know it seems simple, provided you make it your choice to try. One of my favorite quotes from Marilyn Monroe is, "Ever notice how 'What the hell?' is always the right answer?" Make fearless choices to have a great life. Enjoy the adventure, take some chances, learn some lessons the hard way, meet amazing people and learn their views and passions, and develop some of your own.

The choices to make change around us are endless, so what choices will you make to be your own hero? These opportunities can range from saving a life to standing up to a bully, or an unethical workplace situation, to sharing a dream. It's up to you to assess your fear and let it hinder or propel you forward.

So, when it comes to fear and action (or lack thereof), the point is simple. If you do nothing...well, you do nothing. And no one will care. Did you ever read a book about the guy who did nothing, overcame no obstacles, and had no achievements? Yeah, me either, because no one remembers that person, and that story sucks.

Disclaimer:

Just to add a few quick thoughts on fear—while the idea of fears may be imaginary, that doesn't mean that I am trying to say that *danger* is not real. Dangerous situations are genuine, and things like physical and emotional abuse and pain are real. There are things that can still cause you harm or hurt you, like the possibility of an alligator biting my hand when I put my arm in its mouth or lying in a bed of poisonous snakes. You can't positively think your way out of a venomous bite or a vicious attack. So, when it comes to the potential dangers of situations, make choices that work best for your desired outcome. That is, unless you want to get really fucked up, then go for it!

Notes & Thoughts

Notes & Thoughts

CHAPTER 5: SELF-REFLECTION

Who are you? Why do you do things the way you do them? Why are you scared? Why are you so angry? Where does the pain inside you originate? Really, who are you?

Answering such questions amounts to a really hard process for almost all of us. We must slow down our need to react, and to assess why we are doing what we do. When we evaluate a situation, we include the potential consequences of our actions; therefore, we are making a more informed and responsible decision. We are able to determine what good or bad may arise from our decision. How many times do we make a choice and then reap negative outcomes only to say, "Why didn't I think of that?" or "Why did I make this choice?" Slowing down our reaction and assessing the situation allows us to think and recognize the pros and cons of our choices.

I don't mean this about just surface level actions like, "I threw that glass because you made me angry!" I mean the deep down where-did-the-anger originate from level? What happened to you that trained you to become the way you are? Whom or what has hurt you? We all learn, one way or another, to react and respond to different things in different ways from a source that somehow guided us into thinking that the poor ways in which we deal with life are an appropriate way to handle a situation. So, to identify the "why" of your behaviors and reactions, opens up the opportunity to be able to choose different behaviors and reactions. Reflection is a good practice to help us change our habits. When we reflect, we look at the past situation and determine the positive and negative aspects and see what we liked and didn't like about the outcomes. This enables us to be aware of our actions and to change them when a similar situation arises.

Now, I know most therapists will go on a "fun" and, normally, and excruciatingly painful adventure through the particulars of our childhood and parent relationships to find where the need to react with violence or intense emotion started. To their credit, the origins are often insightful, which is much deeper than we ever wanted to go digging. However, it takes us having to play with all the filth and messed up experiences we have tried to forget or have otherwise bottled up for years, putting us back in touch with our skeletons in our long-repressed closet. Although this is a painful endeavor, it is an essential and crucial part of understanding why we make the choices we make and act in the way we do.

Reality check: if you never identify why you developed that reaction, you will never be able to decide to continue or to discontinue it.

What is at the core of why you do the things that you do? Why do you get so defensive? Why do you have so much stubborn pride? Where is the origin of your lack of humility? People fear self-reflection because it forces us to confront the demons that haunt our past. Having to look into ourselves is one of the most difficult things we will ever face. It is much easier to judge others and find faults in them, but to do the same when it comes to ourselves is painful. However, the judgments we have are reflections of the way we judge ourselves. These demons continue to have a dramatic effect on our present and future, and unless you identify them and then make the conscious effort not to do those negative things anymore, you will be doomed to repeatedly live out the same patterns over and over again. Obviously, this is not what you want, and it does not make you feel better about yourself or your life. Identifying the origin of the issue will help you get past that identity of who you are and transition into the person you want to be.

What kinds of demons are we possibly looking at meeting again? One thing is for sure; they can come back. We always have to keep them in check, especially issues such as the root of all "anger issues." Is it from your dad being super strict and angry all the time, or an abusive relationship that changed the way that you responded to life's hiccups? Is it because you didn't get enough love as a kid that you lash out violently to get the attention that you so desperately craved? Is it because your ex and yourself would always fight and yell each other, and that's the only way you feel that you can be heard? Maybe the only way your parents knew how to express themselves was with a smack to the face or by lashing you with a belt, and as a result, the only way you know how to express any kind of solution for something that you have no control over is to smash it or break it. Was it from being bullied? All of these things can create a hurtful place within us which, in turn, cause us to create pain for others. I once heard a saying, "hurt-people hurt people." It is not an echo. I would like to believe people do not intentionally *want* to cause pain to others, but due to our own pain, we present ourselves in a defensive, negative, and abrupt way; this not only causes others to hurt, but it causes us to hurt as well.

Whatever your cause, and regardless of how it became a part of your life, it's yours, and you need to own it. It's uncomfortable to identify root causes because so often we start to rationalize or justify their impact, whether great or small, before we move forward in our self-reflection process. We may have had shitty parents, abusive partners, and terrible influences in our lives, but that is on those people; it does not give us the right to be the same kind of person. Why would we want to turn into the people who hurt us? Is hurting others going to heal our pain? Or is it going to create *more* pain?

When it comes to breaking negative cycles and patterns, we have to make conscious decisions to stop. It's really hard to make conscious decisions about the things we do subconsciously. It takes time and a difficult journey into ourselves through any means we can, but in order to break cycles, self-reflection is a crucial process.

Barriers

One common roadblock to self-reflection is having no outlet to release the stress and pressure that build up throughout life. Finding a proper outlet can help you calm your demons and find the clarity to figure your shit out. Having an outlet is very important, as it gives us a productive way to release the tension we have built up from stress and negativity. Without an outlet, we become agitated and may have angry outbursts. Meditation, music, silence, exercise, therapy, positive affirmations, venting, journaling, dancing, etc., all of these can potentially help you find a way to focus on *you*, so you can understand yourself better. A journal is highly recommended because you are able to look back on your thoughts and feelings and get a better picture of what is happening in your life. After journaling for some time, we are able to see patterns in our emotions and are better able to identify areas we may not have seen before journaling.

I like to think of it as if our minds have a house. We have all these experiences, good or bad, all kept in a metaphorical home, in framed pictures to put on display, or hidden away in dark places we don't talk about or disturb. Let's just say that the dark memories we bottle up are all stored in a closet that you have filled to the top, and you know that if you open the door, those dark things are going to come pouring out in a huge mess with which you don't know how to deal. While it may have remained closed and locked, this full closet starts to have an effect on us in negative ways we don't always understand.

After time, the rotting smell of the festering experiences lingers throughout your house and makes the very air you breathe unbearable and toxic. Your discomfort carries over into your daily life causing such behaviors as: emotional distancing, guarded emotional walls, lack of trust, rage, and insecurities. Some or all of these issues come creeping out of these dark places, shaping us into something we were never meant to be. These emotions or thoughts that are there, for any number of reasons, start to snowball, and against our best intentions, start defining who we are.

We either sabotage a relationship or have a moment where we know we need help. So, we seek advice from friends, from some form of therapy to help us find an outlet in order to quiet the noise in our heads.

It is incredibly hard to reprogram our subconscious reactions to stimuli. We have done things a particular way for so long that to try to change our core programming is like trying to quit a habit cold turkey. It takes a reason to change in order for you to stick with it, but you have to be able to identify the habits you *have* if you are ever going to choose to change them into habits you *want*.

<u>Notes & Thoughts</u>

CHAPTER 6: THE GOLDEN RULE

Now, this is the chapter that seems like the most obvious and easiest to skip. It seems so obvious that I almost left it out myself. But it's the little points we gloss over that impact the bigger picture so much. That said, we have all heard of the Golden Rule, so why devote a chapter to discussing a theory that we all find so simple? Well, we're going to talk about this because while we may understand exactly what it is, we skip over applying it to our lives on a daily basis. So, first, for those of you who may need a refresher:

Treat others the way you would like to be treated.

It seems easy enough, yet why do we not apply this rule to every situation and experience when making choices? If you like encouragement, then encourage somebody else. If you like the way somebody treats you, then treat others that way. If you don't like the way somebody is acting toward you, then don't be that way toward others. If you like being told you're awesome or that you did a fantastic job today, say those kinds of things to other people.

It is so simple, but I believe that one of the main reasons people are in the mindset of doing horrible things or being inconsiderate of others is because the concept of encountering consequence does not seem likely to them. I'll give you an example. I remember once I was in a store, and I saw a small girl, maybe two years old, who was running toward the door to leave the store, and her mom chased her to stop her. The little girl dropped like dead weight. She kicked and screamed and was generally losing her shit in the store. At that moment I realized that the reason that small person was acting in such a manner was because she believed that no matter what did, mom would never leave her. Because of this, she decided she could be absolutely horrible with no risk of facing the consequence that she would be left alone. We behave similarly, if not as ostentatiously. We push the envelope when we don't fear a consequence to our behaviors.

So, the idea of treating others in a way we would like to be treated is generally relative to the perspectives of what we believe is right or wrong or if we believe there are dire consequences or none at all Most people go through life without understanding that there are negative consequences for their actions. They are willing to risk the worst-case scenario but do not accept the likelihood that they could ever suffer negative consequences. But it's important to understand the reason you feel okay with treating somebody the way that you would not like to be treated—you do it because you believe there's no consequences you would suffer that could make your behavior not worth doing. If only we would treat each other with respect, knowing that the worst-case scenario *is* possible, then we could attain a degree of appreciation and care that we would want for ourselves; yet, somehow, it's easier for us to project onto others.

Our life is a series of events that test us and show us our true selves. We may have ideas and theories about how we think the world should be and how people should treat one another, but do we consistently apply and demonstrate those behaviors? How we respond to things and treat other people is a testament to whether we truly believe and live according to our personal ideals of the Golden Rule; or, our responses can tell us if we are just a seemingly intelligent lip service to said rule. The majority of the time, I notice that people don't really know who they are and so they do things in a way they would absolutely hate to see others doing them. So now let's talk about that disconnect or, basically, hypocrisy.

I know we all have situations where we have been guilty of making excuses to not follow this simple rule. There exists a majority of us who can dish it out but sure can't take it. There it is; the "I can't take it," which is what truly reveals how you feel about something. If you can't take the way someone treated you, then you have identified your understanding of your expectations around that behavior or reaction. Need some examples to jog your thinking?

Take the following example: people in relationships pushing expectations, hitting, name-calling, stealing, gossiping, degrading, not showing appreciation, ignoring, cheating, lying, yelling, and/or shunning. The list goes on and on for things being done to us that we don't wish to be returned. Taking the step to make your own list is key in defining your own Golden Rule.

Mirror, Mirror: Reflection First

Let's now get deeper and identify why you do what you do. Take the time to self-reflect. Examine your values, moral code, what drives you, what inspires you, and what it is that you do not give a shit about. All of these go hand-in-hand to define how and why you react to life the way you do. For the purpose of identification, though, it's also about looking at negative situations that make you scream, such as asking, "Why would they do that to someone? They'd hate it if it were done to them!" Well, sorry to say, people have said that about you at some point in your life, so let's talk about why that may have been.

Look at the most recent situations in your life that did not go as smoothly as you wished and pick apart why you reacted the way you did. You can even take the step to ask (and openly receive the feedback) others about areas where you could grow (but remember, you asked, so be ready for answers). Once you understand the what and why behind how you treat others, you can then make the choice to either change it or not. Be consistent or be hypocritical. If you would not like to receive a certain treatment or response, you make a conscious choice to actively stop doing those things. Sounds as easy as a snap of the fingers, right? Well, if you know you are doing something you would not like, it really *is* a conscious choice. Through self-reflection, you take it from your subconscious thought and drag it into the light.

Despite knowing that we are doing something contradictory to treatment we'd want to receive, sadly, we will consciously treat those who are closest to us the shittiest. We rarely argue with friends or acquaintances, yet we can have the shortest fuse with the person we love the most or with whom we share the most. We see it every single day, and you've probably even already seen or done it a few times today—people responding or reacting to someone/thing in a way they have said they would not like having done to themselves. This is the ultimate dismissal of the Golden Rule, and it is why we need to think about it when making choices. It needs to be at the front of your mind at all times, so you don't lash out with hypocritical reactions, especially toward those you love the most.

Golden Pride

Often, regardless of the level of love, we get into an emotionally-fueled altercation with others without thinking of repercussion or consequence. Whether said altercation is treating a customer service representative like trash or yelling at a waitress for a mistake in a food order, saying and doing things that you would not ever want done to you is for some reason justified by some self-fulfilling sense of entitlement. No one owes you! Drop your pride. There is no need to take it out on someone who has little to do with your individual world; argument, altercation, whatever you want to name it. So many are not even necessary for either party.

Dale Carnegie said, "The best way to win an argument is not to have one." Stop trying to win all of the time because, even when you argue your point to be right, the odds are that the other person will not care to hear about it." You damage relationships and friendships over the need to be right, and I would venture to say you personally do not enjoy a know-it-all. Always thinking of the Golden Rule (TGR) will keep you in check regarding what should truly be a fight, if you'd want or welcome it yourself, and how you will consistently respond.

Check Yourself Before You Wreck Yourself

When I question people who are doing something obviously shitty to someone else, it's interesting to see the different reactions. I watch people sift through their methods of justification and avoidance. This is why learning the skills of self-reflection, acceptance and humility makes it easy to be able to stop being an asshole and apologize for doing something you would not like done to you.

I want to point out the fact that some people are just confrontational or difficult, and they *do* expect it back. They revel in bringing others down to their level. Their Golden Rule hardly seems golden. Of course, it's not "right" or "wrong" for them to possibly enjoy the negative treatment if they are being truthful when they say that they do; however, that personality is often created by negative circumstances and positive reinforcement of the negative behavior. Further, if we all got along perfectly, we'd never grow from being hurt or learn the need to approach some people or situations differently. Variety helps us to gain perspective, so embrace the assholes who help you to define how you expect to be treated solidly. When you respond irrationally, even with knowledge of the Golden Rule, you need to stop as soon as you can, even mid-reaction if possible, and go back the tool of self-evaluation to discover why you are reacting that way. Looking outside of yourself with an objective lens, free of excuses and justifications, you can very easily find your reasoning for why you are acting like an asshole. From there, you can refocus your ideas of "do unto others." You expect TGR treatment from others, so you must always have it at the forefront of your mind.

Different Pages

It's challenging to see things from another point of view, but it is impossible when you aren't even trying to; the idea of saying or doing something to hurt someone's feelings is child's play. In most cases, the actions or words we use to hurt are the words that would hurt *us* the most. This is an all-too-common example of projection and TGR dismissal, yet despite a growing self-awareness, it rears its ugly head when a heated moment arises/catches us off guard.

To name some examples, I have seen men degrade women to make them feel weak in an effort to keep themselves from exposing their own insecurity and fear. I have seen women tear into women with insults that don't even apply to the person they are insulting, such as calling a skinny girl fat, a pretty girl ugly, or a smart girl dumb. I have seen people lose it on others over things they cannot even control. I watch people not let others in while merging in traffic. I have seen people fight with words they can't undo or take back. We can all think of example after example of small things that we are willing to use to hurt someone in a way we never want to be hurt. But, for what reason? Having all of those call-outs laid out in front of you, it seems incredibly immature and flat-out wrong that anyone can consciously do these things. However, if we go back to what we discussed earlier in this chapter, everyone has his/her own idea of what the TGR means to and how to apply it. Often when we see such negative behavior we are witnessing the actions of those who have not yet evaluated why they do what they do in order to decide how they feel they should treat others.

To wrap this up, not everyone is on the same page at once, but that's okay. You have to accept this breach of understanding from others with the amount of grace you would want to be given to you and just be solid in your Golden Rule foundations. So, do your homework—self-reflect, define or tweak your personal Golden Rule, ground yourself in your ideas, and live it out. You will stop thinking so much about what others think and gain comfort in the fact that you are treating them as you would like to be treated. Even if your choices seem shitty to others, it is the choice you would want others to make if they were in your shoes. So, you can fall asleep at night at peace, knowing that you aren't a total hypocrite. Making choices in life will become so much easier, I guarantee.

Great Final Chapter Thoughts

It is not about who is right, but what is right.

In many cases, doing the right thing is not the question; the question is—can you recognize that your thoughts and emotions are in control and keeping you from doing what you personally feel to be right? If you are aware (and accepting) of the cost of a bad choice, then, by all means, make your bad choice. If you want a better outcome; treat the situation indifferently, and make a decision based on how you would like things done for you. This seems very hard for many people I interview to do, but if you evaluate the steps we have been through in this book, it is possible! Well...if you choose it to be.

Let's go back to keeping this simple. Don't let fear and stress rule over your choices. Avoid excuses as to why you can't have or do something good for yourself and for others. Trust is the foundation of all healthy relationships. Don't make assumptions or create expectations that are not realistic; you're setting yourself up for disappointment. Learn to understand yourself and why you do what you do. Treat others the way you would like to be treated. Be empowered by the idea that everything you do is a choice. Own the responsibility of your mistakes and learn from them. Move toward your goals, dreams, wants, needs, love, and passions. It's up to *you* to choose, and your actions will help inform your options. Just choose, you powerful creature, you! Choose!

References

Atkinson, William W. (2012). *Thought vibration: or, the law of attraction in the thought world.* Charleston, North Carolina: Nabu Press.

Chapman, G. D. (2010). *The five love languages: how to express heartfelt commitment to your mate.* Bhopal, India: Manjul Pub.

Lin, W., Hu, J. & Gong, Y. (2015). Is it helpful for individuals with minor depression to keep smiling? An event-related potentials analysis. *Social Behavior and Personality.* 43(3), 383-396. Doi:10.2224/sbp.2015.43.3.383

Notes & Thoughts

Notes & Thoughts

Notes & Thoughts

Made in the USA
Columbia, SC
19 December 2022

74537175R00074